THE BREAK-UP BIBLE

101 True Stories To Make You Glad You're Single

THE BREAK-UP BIBLE

101 True Stories To Make You Glad You're Single

By Ruth Graham   Cartoons by Gill Toft

KNOW! THE SCORE

www.knowthescorebooks.com

Know The Score Books Limited
118 Alcester Road
Studley
Warwickshire
B80 7NT
01527 454482
info@knowthescorebooks.com

A CIP catalogue record is available for this book from the British Library   ISBN: 978-1-905449-20-0

Jacket and book design by Lisa David
Cartoons by Gillian Toft

Printed and bound in Great Britain by Cromwell Press, Trowbridge, Wiltshire

Thanks to all the great women who
shared their stories, inspiring me to look
at my own relationship...

And get the hell out of it..

Ruth Graham

6

THE BREAK-UP BIBLE

The perfect antidote to a fresh break-up, a consolation gift for a lonely friend, or just a great way to remind yourself of how life could be a lot worse if you were saddled with some of these charmers!

Inside you'll find a jaw-dropping collection of true anecdotes that will have you breathing a sigh of relief and slipping into your egg-stained dressing gown to sip a glass of Pinot Grigio whilst watching Bridget Jones, grateful that you just don't have to go through this bull**** any more!

Enjoy!!!!

CONTENTS

The Old Testament

How To Spot A Man's Roving Eye   15

Don't Be A Doormat...
He Will Eventually Leave You If...   16

Are You On Your Way To A Break-Up?   18

You're In Denial When...   20

You're Better Off Without Him If...   22

The Good Books

Over Before It Began   27

Slow Realisations   39

Lucky Escapes   47

Embarrassing Endings   63

Hard-Hearted, Mean, Calculating Bastards   71

Bullshit City   79

Foreign Liaisons   85

What A Dick!   93

When The 'Fresh Start' Turns Stale   107

Shallow Be Thy Name   113

Petty Irritations   119

The Joy Of Sex (Or Not!)   125

The New Testament

Ways To Dump The Loser   136

How To Catch A Rat   138

Placatory Mantras   141

Quando rotae aut testes adsunt,
tristitia sequiteur.

(If it's got tyres or testicles – it'll let you down)

THE
OLD TESTAMENT

Is Your Partner Really 100% Committed To You? How To Spot A Man's Roving Eye:

- It's open.

- He goes to the garage for some cigarettes, and clocks up 53 miles in the process.

- He spots a girl in a short skirt and long boots, then sneakily checks to see if you're looking. With the speed of a hummingbird, he looks the other way and back again. However, thanks to peripheral vision, you've seen it all.

- He flirts with the checkout girl at Sainsbury's. And yes – he does need help with his packing, thank you. Trouble is, he's only bought *Nuts* magazine and a pint of milk.

Don't Be A Doormat...
He Will Eventually Leave You If:

- He dances too well. Men like him are in demand – and he knows it.

- You discover he understands the difference between a costume, a bikini, a tankini and a tri-kini – and whether it's a Brazilian, a Hollywood or The Playboy underneath. Yep – he's just got too much of an interest in women.

- He doesn't feel he needs you. Men have to be afraid of losing you to make them behave.

- You don't feel comfortable ever being without make-up. You know subconsciously that he won't fancy you without warpaint. And that's not great.

- You put on half a stone over Christmas and know he will hate it. Shallow bastard!

- You start to look your age. And that age is older than the last girl he really, really fancied.

- He thinks he's a super-hero or a character in Viz.

- Every time you want a relationship check-up or even just an intimate chat, he calls it 'nagging'.

- He has a best friend who womanises and behaves appallingly. Men are easily led. Eventually, the best friend will win.

Are You On Your Way To A Break-Up?

If you fear you are on the verge – check here. Tick three and you are on your way, baby. Harsh, but fair.

• Do you feel the need to check your partner's mobile phone, bank statements, pockets or car mileage? Honey – anyone ever told you, there's a basic lack of trust going on here?

• Do you feel comfortable leaving your partner in the same room as your best friend? Your single, gorgeous, flirtatious best friend?

• Do the words 'darling – I'm just off for a night out with the lads', instil fear into your heart?

• Have you already 'forgiven' him more than twice?

- Did he leave his previous partner for you? The chances are he could do it again.

- Does he claim to 'just love women's company – they're so much nicer to be around than men. But it doesn't mean anything. Honest'.

- Would you seriously put up with the same type of behaviour from a female friend? Eh...?

- The million dollar question. If he was a racehorse, would you honestly put a quid on him?

You Are In Denial When:

- The private detective's report and videos show that he's clearly playing away, but you start to wonder if he has a long-lost twin brother, that just happened to be in town at the same time.

- He propositions the private detective, but you put it down to his 'charm'.

- You fantasise together about having a threesome. The next day he's been on the internet and gone ahead with it... without you, saying he wanted to road-test the dynamics. And, yes, you're right, maybe it shouldn't be with two girls, but possibly another couple, the next time.

- He says he loves you, but men were genetically meant to spread their seed... there's just nothing he can do about it (followed by an apologetic shrug).

- You're pretending that monosyllabic conversations and evenings in front of the TV are 'just what marriage turns into. It's no big deal'.

- He's let you down several times for 'unexpected important events' that he never actually mentions again.

- His aunty has died more than twice.

You're Better Off Without Him If:

- He can't cook, clean, iron or make a meal. Who needs a 13 stone baby anyway?

- He's over 40 and still waiting for the big time: the next audition, that possible showcase, the big break. He's a liability – dump him!

- He talks bitterly about his ex. Either he's a woman-hater, or he still loves her.

- He's had over 100 women. There's only so much beaver a man can brave before he becomes addicted.

THE
GOOD BOOKS

OVER BEFORE IT BEGAN

These are the ones that limp to get past, or even reach, the first date.

It's the curled lip around the soup spoon, the whining accent you know you couldn't live with, the parting with dandruff in it or the addiction to old episodes of **The A Team**. *Whatever it is you hate, once you've spotted it, it's gonna be hard to ignore.*

Nothing Martina could do would drag Vince away from the sports pages.

A friend of a friend told me about this guy called Neil at work, who was apparently very nice. She told him about me too, and passed on both sets of numbers. I called for a preliminary chat, and it soon became apparent that he'd had a personality bypass.

After a huge gap, I asked him what his hobbies were. He replied "conversation", followed by another big silence. I tried another tack, asking him what his plans for the future were. He said none, as he'd been feeling suicidal lately, so didn't want to look too far forward!

~ **Reena, London**

My blind date came to pick me up in his car – a mustard-yellow coloured thing. I came out of the house, he rolled down his window and smiled.

My first (horrified) thought was that his teeth matched the paintwork! Ugh!!!!!!

~ **Jenny, Ilfracombe**

I met an American guy on holiday who seemed very nice, and I thought we may have had a future.

However, it was clear we didn't when, at the end of the week, he offered to fly me out to see him in Arkansas, adding, "and while you're there, my plastic surgeon could get your legs fixed up in no time!"

Bloody cheek!

~ **Sarah, Preston**

First date. Salsa dancing. Wrong time of the month. White skirt. Nobody told me. Say no more...

~ **Sacha, Birmingham**

My first internet date was eventful. I went up to Birmingham to meet Ian, who looked good on the website and had been a great talker for the couple of weeks prior to us meeting.

Things were fine until I got off the train to be met by a grinning man with no front teeth... I hadn't noticed that all his pictures had showed him smiling, but with his mouth closed.

~ **Caroline K, London**

It's flattering to date a younger man, but I smelt the coffee on our second date, when he had to ring up his dad to check if it was OK to stay overnight at my house. Oops!

~ **Sadie, Ipswich**

I was on a first date with a guy, which seemed to be going well. Halfway through dinner, he picked up his glass and said he was off to the bathroom.

I waited, and waited for him to come back, feeling more conscious than ever that I was alone at the table, especially as there were people I knew in the restaurant.

Eventually, I realised that he'd picked up his glass. Doh! He'd had no intention of coming back, and it had taken me 25 minutes to realise.

I quietly paid the bill and slunk out, with my self-esteem on the floor.

~ Linsi, Sussex

I knew it was over when he picked me up wearing a pink shirt. Full stop.

~ Sophie P, London

I met a much younger man, who wouldn't believe that I was considerably older than him. I was almost flattered into accepting a date, but just as I was doing so, he described me (to my face), as a 'fit bitch'. I knew then that the generation gap was too wide!

~ Morag, Carlisle

Jenny knew the future looked bleak, as the arthritis in her elbows did not allow her to 'high-five' her toyboy.

After being single for ages, I went speed dating, but every date was hideous, starting with the first guy, Mark. He had a full boil on the face, thick black specs, and was wearing a cagoule. He seemed pleasant enough, but someone should advise him that the best way to impress on a date isn't to admit (within 30 seconds) that "half my insides are missing, actually".

I then asked him if he'd ever been a member of our local action/adventure club that people use heavily to find new friends and dates. He responded that it was a bit too adventurous; due to his missing insides he couldn't do any of the action things, and he couldn't eat the curries on their gourmet nights. Never has three minutes seemed so long!

– **Penny, Birmingham**

I have bad stretch marks on my lower stomach, but look OK when I'm dressed. When I took my clothes off for the first time, my then boyfriend visibly recoiled.

He tried to hide it, but I could tell he was (in the words of *Sex And The City*) 'just not that into me', and we never got past the starting blocks.

~ **Louise, Hammersmith**

I met a very sexy man who invited me back to his for coffee.

I made myself comfortable on the sofa, but when he reappeared he had indeed made coffee, but also managed to change into a pair of tartan old men's slippers.

I did snog him, but out of the corner of my eye I kept seeing these tartan slippers and it really put me off.

~ **Kathy, Sutton Coldfield**

Tartan slippers! Only a penis the size of the Eiffel Tower could save things now.

First impressions really count, so I made sure I looked immaculate for my blind date.

I stepped off the train, spotted him from his description immediately and walked towards him, hoping he liked the look of me. When we got face to face, I expected him to shake my hand, or kiss me on the cheek. However, he simply cupped both of his hands, and plonked them firmly onto the point of my breasts!

Without uttering a sound, I stepped backwards, resumed walking, and got straight back onto the train. The total 'exchange' between us had lasted precisely five seconds. A record, surely?

~ **Silke, Hamburg**

38

SLOW REALISATIONS

Ooooh – not a nice one. This is the moment when the realisation crawls all over you that it's finally over. Sadly, there's more chance of salvaging the Titanic...

Lorraine wondered whether to start eating or give Tom just five more minutes to get home?

When my best friend sent me a very serious letter, detailing 100 reasons why I shouldn't be with my boyfriend, it dawned on me that I was being an idiot, and all the crap, crass things he did and said were so wrong for me.

I hated her for pointing them out to me, but in retrospect, it was the kindest thing she could have done. And we're still mates, while he was kicked to the kerb years back.

– Yvette, Bournemouth

I was entertaining some very highbrow dinner party guests from the local university, so the talk was fairly intellectual. We moved on from astronomy to theatre, via Shakespeare and Brecht, before my Italian boyfriend, who was obviously feeling left out, piped up "I saw a musical once". I nearly died.

– Liz, Solihull

I didn't know it was exactly over, but it was the beginning of the end when our pet parrot suddenly squawked "God I want to **** you Julie".

I'm a born-again Christian, and would never allow language like that in the house. But my friend Julie isn't. And the parrot had got my husband's voice to a T!

~ **Cheryl, Hull**

You can often tell a lot about somebody by their friends, so I got that sinking feeling the first time I went out for dinner with my boyfriend and his mates and their partners.

Halfway through the meal, the guy to the left of me leaned over and said, "do you think you could get this bottle up you?"

I was horrified!

~ **Lesley, Kent**

My boyfriend Stu was lovely, but thick.

He was an electrician, and I was a law tutor at the local university, so we struggled to find common ground.

However, the sex was really good, so I consoled myself with that. But holding a conversation was extremely difficult, and it worried me.

When I suggested he read books, or studied something outside of work, he'd fix me with a bemused look as if to say, "ah bless her – she's trying again", and then say, "You know your problem, love. You just think too much. Come and sit down and watch Garfield with me".

My heart plummeted, imagining future years spent with my brain on slow, sitting on the sofa, eating sweeties and watching cartoons. I finished it the next morning.

– **Ruth, Birmingham**

Something wasn't right about the chemistry with Ken, so it had to finish. And then I realised that maybe it was the droopy chest, due to previous nipple piercings and the fact that he'd had a belly button piercing too. Odd I thought...

~ **Charlotte K, Warwick**

After looking forward to a weekend away for ages, I was mortified when my boyfriend invited his mother! Not only that, but he booked his mum and I a twin room to share, while he had his own.

It was strained to say the least, and it was most definitely all over by the time he dropped me home.

~ **Katie, Nottingham**

I knew it was (finally) over, when I sat sobbing on my boyfriend's doorstep, 10 minutes after he'd finished with me. He sent me a text saying, "Go. Away. Now. Or I will throw a bucket of water on you".

~ **Claire, Hounslow**

I was seeing a guy in Alaska – Steve. He and I dated for five years, but even when I moved to the USA, he visited twice, as did I.

Then, he just stopped communicating. I mean dead in my tracks stopped. From everyday calls, texts and e-mails, to... nothing.

I called, I e-mailed, I wrote letters. I called friends of his to make sure he was OK, but never ever heard another word from him or found out what happened.

Three years later when my mother died, I received the most beautiful card and letter from him about how fortunate he was to meet her and what a wonderful person she'd been and how bad he felt about my loss.

Not a word about me!

~ Debbie, Ventura, California

LUCKY ESCAPES

You know you've had a lucky escape when you look back on the relationship (or brief encounter), and the emotions are either sheer relief that it's over, or cold horror that you slept with a man you probably, in saner moments, wouldn't even have lent your car to.

Carol sighed when she thought of what might have been.

47

I was very young (about 17), dating a much older, very polite gentleman. To impress him, I took him back to meet my mum for afternoon tea.

It started off well, but as he relaxed, he changed personality. At some stage after the sandwiches, he told a very rude joke containing references to women, and Grimsby fish market. Me and mum didn't know where to look.

But it got much worse when he farted loudly, sniffed the air and said, "Ooh – you could put a tail on that!"

Mum looked so disgusted, I knew I could never, ever see him again.

~ **Alex, Birmingham**

I'm from an older generation that had obedience drummed into us, but I'm ashamed to admit that my husband used to buy our groceries wholesale, then he'd lock them in the larder and charge me retail prices from my housekeeping allowance.

I left him one day when he'd gone to the warehouse to re-stock.

~ **Linda, Norfolk**

My newish boyfriend told me to dress up for Friday night, as he was taking me to a club. So, I dressed in a black halterneck, false eyelashes, glitter make-up, killer heels – the works. I nearly died when we arrived at the venue, only to realise it was the local working men's club!

I spent the evening with a lager and a bag of pork scratchings in my hand, hating him and wanting the evening to finish so I could dump him when he dropped me home.

~ **Ruth, Birmingham**

I dated a guy in Wales. Every time I went there, it was like a state visit. His mother would get out the best china, wave it at me, and say "whoever marries our Carl gets the Harlequin Tea Service".

I couldn't bear it. Their lives were sooooooo small.

~ **Cassie, Brighton**

My boyfriend was unhealthily obsessive about everything from checking he'd locked his car door to folding down the bedsheets with an exact crease.

I couldn't stand it any more when I caught him writing dates in his diary. "What are you doing?" I said. His reply was that he was logging all the food in the cupboard, and their sell-by dates to make sure anything I made for him was fresh!

Well, next on the menu was goodbye-pie!

~ **Fiona, Boston**

I spent one lovely sunny afternoon in a wine bar, in a friend's home town. Looking for somewhere to sit, I ended up cramming myself onto the edge of a table full of guys and after a couple of drinks I got talking to one who seemed pretty nice and friendly (and, I thought, cute).

One drink led to another, and another and we were getting on so well that I had a 'Cosmo mag independent woman moment' and invited him the following Friday to come and stay with me for the night.

As the day approached I did start to worry that maybe he wasn't as cute as I'd thought, due to my beer goggles, but reasoned 'Oh well, he definitely wasn't ugly and we had got on, so it couldn't be that bad, could it?' And who knew – maybe this could be the start of something wonderful?

So, I'd arranged to meet him at the local train station rather than direct him to my house, and I thought we could go to the local pub first to break any ice.

A week later, right on time, his car approached and my heart immediately dropped... I could barely see him over the steering wheel!

As his door opened and he got out I realized in that split second that I had not seen him get up to go to the bathroom at all during our conversation the previous week, so I had no idea on build, height etc. In fact he barely made 5ft, to the point that – if I was totally honest I – doubt that he even made 4 feet 10 inches !!!!!!!!!

I'm no towering glory myself, but at 5 feet 6 inches I do generally like my guys to be able to kiss me without getting on a box.

Well, I figured I would have to go for a drink with him and let him down gently, maybe the old 'I've recently come out of a relationship and I'm not looking for another one', would work.

I did try a number of tactics over the evening which I thought were sinking in and as he'd had a few drinks I decided to myself that I would have to let him stay... in the spare bed!

After we got home I showed him where he was sleeping and went to the bathroom. I can still remember the shock on walking back into my bedroom and seeing him standing in the middle of the room stark naked.

However it wasn't his birthday suit that shocked me, nor was it seeing him full height, it was the fact that his entire body was covered in Warner Bros. characters, with both nipples pierced!

There wasn't a single character missing, and I think seeing Sylvester on one buttock and Tweetie Pie on the other made me realize it was all over!!

~ Catherine, Stafford

It was over the second I checked my boyfriend's phone, only to find a text to someone referring to me as 'the bint'.

– **Charlotte, York**

They say it's the thought that counts, but I didn't think much of the cigarette lighter (from Asda), that my husband gave me for my 32nd birthday.

Yep – I guess that was the moment the flame went out for me!

– **Ann, Birmingham**

Every birthday, and every Christmas, and every Valentine's day, my partner bought me gifts, which always included stockings and suspenders, or leather-wear, basques and the like. I never wore them, as I have a stomach I'm embarrassed about, but no matter how many times I told him, there were always more.

I realised that the stockings were a metaphor for our relationship, and it was all about what he wanted, not me, so I finished it.

Years later, on a night out with friends, I bumped into him again. In a gay club, wearing some of my old 'presents'.

Nice, eh?

~ Carol, Derby

I knew it was really all over for us when – I started smiling again!

To explain – my partner of 16 years was an alcoholic, which caused me to lose all my confidence. I stayed for our children, but was deeply unhappy. Then, a childhood friend of mine came into my life, and encouraged me to go out with her.

As the months went by, I had fun, took more care of myself, and started to get noticed again. One night, Tony was working away, and called to say goodnight. I explained I was going "off to bed" any minute – when really I was about to hit the town!

Needless to say, my girlfriends were laughing away in the background... and I didn't feel remotely guilty. I kind of realised that if I was lying to him, then for sure he was doing the same to me!

It was only a matter of months before we finally parted, and I've never looked back!

I'm now married again, blissfully happy and love life. I'd advise anyone 'stuck in a rut' to get out of it and not allow fear to paralyse you. There are lovely men out there – you just have to be available and free of all your baggage.

I was in my late 30s when I took the plunge to move on... and so glad I was able to turn my life around!

– Jackie C D, Birmingham

My much-loved boyfriend announced he was looking forward to being a father. But 'probably not' with me. I was staggered at the realisation that we had no future.

But that was 10 years ago, time heals, and we've both gone on to have kids with other partners. Our children do go to the same school, though thankfully, it's not my kids that are now referred to as 'the ginger hobbits in year four'.

~ Fiona, West Midlands

I got back from a holiday, and my dad told me my boyfriend had called six times that week, to see if I was home yet. I was thrilled – he'd missed me!

But, apparently not. He'd only been so keen to call because he'd met someone else, and was dying to finish it. I was gutted.

He went on to marry the girl, but it only lasted a year, due to his outrageous mood swings. The very ones I'd put up with for a year, convincing myself it was just a phase. Thank goodness she took him off my hands.

~ Rachel, Perth, Australia

Back in the mid '90s, I wasn't as wise as I am now, but even then I knew it was a total cheek, when my boyfriend finished the relationship, saying he "had to get more experience" before he settled down.

"But," he added, "if it doesn't work out with Laura, I'd like to come back to you."

What a complete drain!!

~ **Charlotte, Birmingham, Alabama**

Meanness is so unattractive, and I used to hate it when my boyfriend hung back when it was his round. Saying he was "full", he'd shake his head and say "no – it's OK. You go ahead mate." to whoever was next in line.

This happened not once, but every time. Eventually, friends stopped inviting us out, and that was when I knew he had to go.

~ **Sarah, Leicester**

I was having an affair (OK – nobody's perfect), and his wife rang while we were at the pub one lunchtime. After the phone call, he instantly leaped up and said, "I've got to go".

"Oh," I said, "is it something important at home then?"

"Yes," he replied, "she's just called to say the blender's broken down. So I've got to go and get her a new one."

I gave up on the spot, knowing that if he'd go for such a petty reason, I'd always, but always, take second place.

~ **Eliza R, Manchester**

I knew it was over when my boyfriend announced that living with me had driven him to join the Catholic church.

He'd secretly been meeting a priest for two hours a week for the past year, and had made the decision to join the priesthood full-time.

However, before he left, he asked if we could have wild sex one last time. I told him to go and find a choirboy!

~ **Lucy, Walton-on-Thames**

I got up one morning and found my boyfriend in his dressing gown and a pair of rubber gloves, looking very harassed.

"What are you doing?" I said.

"Bleaching," he responded curtly. "I've been fretting all night and had to get up and start. Since you moved in, it's filthy. Just filthy."

I knew I couldn't live with that a second longer.

~ Emma, Los Angeles

I met a man in a nightclub, who spent 25 minutes chatting me up, giving me all the lines about how nice he was, how well he treated women, how he was looking for a woman to spoil and love etc.

Which was lovely, except for the fact that we'd slept together just two weeks beforehand, and he obviously had no recollection of me at all.

~ Tinneka, Amsterdam

EMBARRASSING ENDINGS

There's nothing like an embarrassing end to a relationship to provide great dinner party fodder. But don't expect to pull anyone new around the table when you're sharing these stories. You have been warned.

Having lusted after sporty Brian for months, Jane realised this probably wasn't the ideal time to be caught short.

It was all over for me when I took my clothes off for the first time in front of Neil. Without a trace of irony, he leaped off the bed and made for the door, muttering, "Oh damn. I forgot to set the video for *Fat Friends*"!

~ **Ruth, Birmingham**

I had alopecia, and my confidence was at an all-time low, so I was amazed that I managed to 'pull' a fit guardsman who worked for the Queen.

A few dates later, I had to pop out to the shops, but came back after just 10 minutes, as I'd forgotten my purse. And there he was – my fit guardsman, lying on the bed in my basque, full make-up, and my other wig.

I couldn't stand the thought that he'd just dated me for my spare hair.

~ **Julie, Coventry**

I stood in the middle of a pub, watching my boyfriend, drunk and out of control, holding a pint of beer on his head, singing 'These Are The Decadent Days'. He looked such an idiot.

That was the defining moment after which I knew we'd got no future.

~ **Pauline, Edinburgh**

I went to see my new boyfriend for the evening, and after a lovely dinner and some TV, we decided to walk the dog about 9pm.

Before going out, I visited the bathroom, as I was having a very heavy cycle and wanted to check my tampon situation. My boyfriend went in after me, but a few seconds later, came hopping out, shrieking his head off.

On the bottom of his foot was a huge blood clot. It must have fallen out of me onto the floor during the change, and was so big, you could have put wheels on it and believed it was a skateboard! Horrific!!

I die thinking about this now, and his total and utter disgust.

From his reaction – I just knew it was over.

– Dana, Michigan, USA

The signs were there when my partner and I were on holiday in Amsterdam.

During a visit to a sex shop, we bought some love beads for him, but I didn't want to spend the extra Euro on a little pull cord that would make it easier to remove them!

When we used them that night, needless to say, they got stuck inside him, and he spent fifteen minutes straining on the toilet, trying to push them out.

He was really annoyed, and I was really put off, and it fizzled out from there.

~ Justine, Birmingham

Things had not been too great on the sex front for several months, so one morning I decided to give my boyfriend a surprise before he went to work by coming downstairs wearing just high heels and a feather boa.

As I entered the sitting room, I saw he was on the telephone. He looked up, gave me a cursory glance, turned away and carried on talking about computers. I slinked back upstairs, feeling incredibly foolish.

~ Ruth, Birmingham

Holiday romances are a great excuse to behave out of character, which I was very prepared to do with this gorgeous man I met in Morocco.

I was on a tour, so only had one night to make my move. I left the rest of the group, and went off to dinner with Ali at his uncle's carpet shop, where we ate lots of tagine and couscous.

It was lovely, but after about half an hour, I felt my stomach churning, and knew I needed the loo. What followed was the worst bout of food poisoning ever. The toilet was only feet away from where we'd been eating, so he must have heard everything.

I was so, so embarrassed, I could hardly leave the bathroom, and had to phone the tour leader to come and get me. Aaargh!

~ **Elspeth, Edinburgh**

I went right off my normal remit and had sex with a hippy once. We didn't know each other that well, but it was a shock when we had sex and he became another person.

Although we used a condom, he absolutely freaked out at the fact there was a speck (literally) of my blood on it. First of all he was disgusted, then he asked me to sit on a sheet of plastic(!), and then he said the blood had gone on his stomach, and would bring up a past life experience.

It was all too weird by now, so I dressed quickly and left his tent, with the words "Oh God. It's starting. I don't know how I'm going to process this," ringing in my ears.

~ Sarah, Bognor Regis

HARD-HEARTED, MEAN, CALCULATING BASTARDS

Nobody deserves more than one encounter with idiots like these. These men are sent to learn from – not lean on.

Jonathon knew that if he argued hard enough, Michelle would have an asthma attack and pass out, giving him the perfect opportunity to sneak off and meet Denise.

I had been married three years, and seeing as we worked very hard at our jobs in Kenya, I was looking forward to relaxing on holiday in the USA.

However, my husband arranged for us to spend the entire six week break in our old home town of Birmingham. I couldn't understand it – everyone had moved on, and all there was were my parents.

The moment we landed, he started being vile to me, not wanting to do anything or go anywhere. It turned out he'd met someone in Kenya, and had decided to bring me home and literally dump me back where he'd found me. This would mean I'd lose my home, my job and all my friends, in one fell swoop.

Despite my horror, I held things together, and insisted on returning to tie up loose ends. I figured that if I was out there, at least it would make it difficult for him to have this affair under my nose.

Turns out I was wrong. Despite me being there, he simply dropped my bags out of the cab when we got to Kenya, and went straight over to his lover's. They moved in together that night and carried on their affair, right under my nose.

~ **Katy, Birmingham**

I went to the local B&Q to pick up some double wardrobes I'd ordered, only to find they had been cancelled a week ago and replaced with an order for a single wardrobe.

I phoned home to see if my partner could explain, but the phone just rang out... When I got back, there was an explanatory note that a double wardrobe was 'no longer necessary', accompanied by the number of a DIY man to help me build the single.

How thoughtful.

~ **Lara, Isle of Wight**

I flew all the way to Australia to visit a guy I'd met on holiday the year before, but even though I was in his house he acted very, very cool with me.

Turned out he'd met someone in the interim and hadn't the nerve to tell me, so he'd sent her on a holiday to my home town in the UK, while I was out there.

Worse, it took his mate to tell me the truth.

~ **Leanne, Bolton**

I thought it would be lovely to renew our marriage vows, but my Italian husband seemed quite evasive.

I told my friend, who was studying Italian at college, and she said she'd come round to help make preliminary enquiries to move things along.

I put on some coffee and handed her my wedding certificate as a starting point. "Oh God," she said, "I'm really sorry, but this isn't a marriage certificate. You've never actually been married."

That complete bastard had taken me to Rome 15 years previously, made me participate in an intimate ceremony (I'd wondered why he wanted just us and a friend present), and then I'd signed a 'friendship' agreement.

No wonder he was being evasive – there were no 'vows' to renew!

– **Margaret, Twickenham**

After 20 years of marriage, and three children, I discovered my husband had not one mistress, not two, but three!!!

One was black, one was Chinese and one was Asian – it was like the League of Nations. And every one of them was set up in their own apartment, along with their (his) respective children.

It almost finished me, and it broke my heart to think of the times he'd left family occasions and holidays early, saying he'd got to go and 'work' (he's a songwriter – and people marry and make love to his work every day – it makes me sick).

I was devastated when I found out, but have since found myself again – I'd always been overshadowed by his fame, so in a way, I'm happy.

– Kesi, Sydney

My mum was dying in a hospice and I got a call that morning to say come now, she's not got long to last. I packed a bag and prepared to drive the 100 miles to Birmingham.

My boyfriend packed his bag too, but it was for a bridge weekend in Suffolk. He left before me, barely glancing back over his shoulder, saying to "give him a ring if there was any news."

And there was. Once I buried my mum, he was dumped.

~ Alice, Bromley

BULLSHIT CITY

These relationships make Paris Hilton look sincere. Listening to all their bullshit has faded their attraction, worn you out and (worst of all) made you feel foolish in front of your mates (who will have clocked it months ago, and be wondering what on earth you see in him).

79

Being mad about someone is never a good thing, as you tend to make excuses for them. This was the case with Rob, my partner. Even though I was in my early 30s, I was still gullible enough to believe it when he told me he was a secret service agent.

After a year of him disappearing and letting me down to go on 'secret' missions, I finally realised it was over when I went into the loft in search of a leak, and found stacks of books and stuff off the internet about how to be a spy, along with tons of notes in a little book, detailing all his 'jobs' (which were obviously made up).

Oh yes – and a hole he'd drilled through to our 25 year-old neighbour's attic conversion, which allowed him to see straight into her bedroom.

~ **Karine, Finland**

I was attracted to Ace for his alternative views and lifestyle. Very green, very right-on, we spent a summer together, going to festivals when we could, eating organic, living in his van and doing all the 'right' things.

But then all the mystery disappeared when I discovered he was actually a 36 year-old trolley dolly, called Nigel, who was having a sabbatical from work and living with his parents.

~ **Alex, Chicago**

My boyfriend always used his cat as an excuse to stand me up. The first time, he couldn't come out, as it had been pack-raped. Apparently.

And then about a week later, he stood me up again saying he had to stay in and look after it, because as a result of the 'rape' it had caught chlamydia.

To this day, I'm still not sure whether he was lying or not.

~ **Heidi, Frankfurt**

I was at a very posh dinner party, seated at the end of a rectangular table. Either side of me were two very pompous (English) businessmen, who made it their business to talk in French, purposely to exclude and belittle me.

My partner was at the other end of the table, perfectly aware of what an awful time I was having, eating my dinner in silence and being ignored. I got angrier and angrier that he didn't intervene or change seats, and by the end of the meal, I was ready to burst, so I stood up – and told the men what I thought of them (it was surreal, almost like someone else speaking)... the table fell silent, but I was in full swing.

I informed one that his wife was having an affair, that everyone around the table hated them and especially loathed their spoilt pony-riding, money grabbing, pretentious, buck-toothed children.

And then I told the other that friends always poured his gifts of home-made wine down the sink after he'd gone.

After my tirade, I simply excused myself from the table, and went to order a cab, knowing that my relationship was SOOOOOO over, and that I'd never be 'welcome' in their (hideous, pretentious) social circle again.

~ **Penny, Southend**

A boyfriend had insisted we did not need to use contraception, as apparently he'd been in the Royal Marines during the Falklands War and he'd been shot in his testicles, which had rendered him infertile.

Imagine how horrified I was to discover a few months later that, not only was he married, but his wife was 12 weeks pregnant!

Turned out he was an utter, compulsive liar, and had never even graduated from army training camp.

~ **Karen, West Sussex**

FOREIGN LIAISONS

It's all very exciting on holiday, but teaming up with a foreign man is a bit like buying a dress; looks nice in the shop window, but doesn't always go with what you've got at home.

Fiona prayed that eventually Neasden would rub off slightly on Abamadu.

I was kissing a Greek waiter on holiday, when he told me that he wanted to "kiss me in the district".

I thought he meant something very sexy, but he actually just meant outside, in the courtyard, by the bins. Not classy!

~ **Lin, Plymouth**

It's cringeworthy now, but I fell for a musician in one of those Mariachi bands that play for tourists. This was in Rome, many years ago, and rather than enjoy my holiday, I ended up following him round for two weeks, helping him and the band sell their cassette tapes, whilst watching him flirt with tourists.

He turned up for 'work' one day in a brightly knitted shawl and a large hat, and I tried to envisage him in Stevenage with me, but couldn't. That was the moment realisation struck.

~ **Ella, Herts**

The Germans aren't renowned for their sense of humour, and even though Marco was diluted by being Swiss German, it didn't make it any better. And the worst thing was – he thought he was really funny. Mix Alan Partridge and David Brent with a Germanic accent, and you're somewhere close.

After every statement he'd exclaim "HOOOOOLY COW!!" really loudly (thinking this was cool). And he'd say (in his very robotic voice) – "Wow – You English are so craaaazeeeee" – even when it was something really normal like having a chaser before a pint.

I endured two visits before sending him on his way.

~ **Tess, Birmingham**

The Italians have a saying – 'keep to your own women, and your own cows', and now I know why.

I dated an Italian, but because of the language barrier, we never really had a laugh. I really missed having humour in the relationship, and any laughs were me laughing at him, not with him.

I laughed at the letter saying he "loved beautiful English girl with blue eye", but the day he sent me a letter promising to buy me "a very set of undies" and to "hamp me very strang", I knew it simply couldn't go on, so it was best to bale out.

I never discovered what 'to hamp' really meant.

~ **Kerry, Ireland**

I met a beautiful Frenchman, who could speak no English. My French wasn't so great, so I set myself the task of learning, before his first visit to England.

I studied intensely for several weeks, and really grasped the basics by the time he came over. Do you know, he didn't even comment on all the effort I'd made! He didn't even appear to notice. And he let me pay for everything. And he had the most appalling wind I've ever encountered, which again, he didn't feel the need to comment on.

I finished the relationship (in French!), and waved him off after the weekend, knowing it was the most over of any over relationships I have ever had.

– **Ruth, Birmingham**

I used to go out with a Moroccan, but couldn't stand it when he used to put on his little woven, pointy shoes, and pirouette round on his toes with his mates. He just looked such a twat.

~ Jenny, Devon

WHAT A DICK!

Whether it's lying and cheating, using people or just being hard as nails – they're all here. Oh, and a quick warning – you might need a teaspoon of sugar before delving into this motley bunch. Or is it just me that detected the teeniest, weeniest hint of bitterness here...

As a surprise, I went to the airport to meet my boyfriend from his holiday.

Heart all a-flutter, I watched his plane land, I watched the steps reach the plane, the door open... and my boyfriend descend, hand-in-hand with his (supposedly) ex-girlfriend.

That was my decisive moment.

~ **Avril, St Etienne**

I knew it was over one Christmas when I walked in on my husband kissing the au pair, as they were wrapping presents in the sitting room.

I fired her and sent her back to Sweden, but she still had the nerve to ring up and wish us all a Happy New Year!

~ **Penny, Sussex**

I'm still angry now, years later, that my then (wealthy) boyfriend allowed me to sign up and be a guinea pig in a drugs trial, just so I had enough to pay my bills.

Over six weeks, I suffered 10 induced asthma attacks and then had my throat frozen and a tube inserted through my nose, to take a scraping from my lung.

I vomited during this, my nose bled on and off for a week, and I earned just £650 – just about what he charges for half a day as a motivational speaker.

– Pauline, London

There's nothing more sobering than clearing out your mother's effects, only to find a love letter in her personal files... from your own husband.

It finished my relationship, but I never found out if she responded; and it's too late now.

The only saving grace was that the letter was filed under 'miscellaneous'.

– Tanya, Cape Town

I knew it was over on a skiing holiday, when I found my husband in bed with a friend of ours. They'd left me and her husband on the slopes, and sloped off unnoticed.

If I hadn't needed something from the chalet, they wouldn't have been found out. When I walked in, they were under the sheets, but still had their clothes on, so they tried to convince me they were just 'trying to keep warm'.

– **Ali, Derbyshire**

My boyfriend and I went through university together and were pretty much love's young dream, but he was SO handsome (and vain), that it was inevitable he'd be unfaithful eventually.

This happened, during a break three years later when I went to London and I discovered he had started sha**ing a friend of a friend. So then we were apart for a few months but we got back together, but I was always insecure.

One day, this random girl approaches me in the street and tells me that her sister has been sha**ing my boyfriend for the last 12 months. Turns out her sister was the 'friend of a friend', and he'd never stopped seeing her. But while I knew nothing, she knew all about me, where I worked, etc etc... AND she had gotten pregnant by my boyfriend. Nice.

He took her to get an abortion behind my back, but they carried on sha**ing. I also found out that they had never once used contraception of any kind. Great – exactly what he and I were doing (I was on the Pill though).

It turned out that he used to be at my house 'with me' until 11pm, but he couldn't stay owing to my strict parents. So then he would drive to her place afterwards and be with her. Brilliant. I never had a clue and this went on for a year.

Anyway the best thing was that I'd had a job interview for a PR role in London a few weeks before

I found out exactly what had been going on. He was typically unimpressed, discouraging me, telling me I wouldn't get it. How wrong...!

Literally within three weeks of me finding out that he was a complete prick, I had packed up my whole life and moved to London; binning him and getting myself a new life.

Ha ha!!! (Not that I'm bitter!)

~ **Joanna L, London**

My relationship was over the Saturday night I switched on the television to watch *Blind Date,* and was stunned to see my boyfriend on it – as the 'picker'!

– **Sophie C, Tooting**

Sandy was so horrified to see her lover on Blind Date that she ended up eating her own bodyweight in Pringles.

I knew my relationship was over when I got a call from a young sales girl from a local department store. She brightly informed me that the shirt my husband and I had been looking for last week was now in stock.

When I said you must have the wrong customer she said, "No, you remember you were in with your husband, Bill, looking at shirts. I helped you both pick out some shirts and ties".

When I said I hadn't been in that store for months, she got very flustered and then fell silent.

My heart sank.

– **Yvonne, California**

One day, my boyfriend (who I adored, and thought I knew well), sat down and said that he couldn't lie to me anymore. I actually laughed, thinking he was mucking about, but no. Amidst lots of tears, he then unloaded his guilt, along with the story of how, in our 14 months together, he'd visited prostitutes, had nine affairs, and even managed to squeeze in a homosexual relationship too!!!!

I went through every emotion under the sun in seconds – from horror to revulsion to devastation. Then I calmly picked up my bag and began packing it.

He rushed into the sitting room, and the next thing I heard was music. Can you believe he'd put on The Bangles' song, 'Eternal Flame'.

The man was insane.

~ **Ruth, Birmingham**

My husband gave me scabies and was very indignant when I discovered it, saying it must have been me not changing our bedroom sheets often enough.

~ Julie, Salzburg

I knew it was over the morning I rang my boyfriend, to see what time he was coming to pick me up for our Easter weekend away.

His girlfriend answered his mobile, saying he'd spent the night at hers, as he wanted to see his baby son.

I hadn't known either the girlfriend, or the child, existed.

– **Justine, Solihull**

Working on a passenger cruise liner is the ideal way to meet people, but relationships don't last long as it's very transient.

I felt with Daryl I had something different though, and we spent every moment possible together. He even asked me to disembark with him at the end of our contract, and begin a new life in Vancouver (where he came from).

But I realised it was over just two weeks before we began this 'new life', when I got a letter from a 'wellwisher', telling me that Daryl already lived with a woman in Vancouver, and had another girlfriend on another ship too. And I'd wondered why, on our day off in port, he never wanted to go out with me.

~ **Tanya, Fort Lauderdale**

I was giving my lovely new boyfriend some oral relief, when a picture of his previously unmentioned, six month-old baby, fell from his trouser pocket.

It was over for me before he ejaculated...

~ **Harriet, Warwickshire**

WHEN THE 'FRESH START' TURNS STALE

If you seriously doubt that men and women were ever really meant to live together, these are for you.

Despite his best efforts Dan would never get it right. Apparently, tampons weren't a 'proper' present.

When my marriage hit the rocks after my husband's affair, we decided to try again with a second honeymoon in the Caribbean. I tried so hard to impress, lost weight, dressed beautifully – everything I knew.

However, I conceded defeat the afternoon that I climbed into the enormous hot tub on our hotel's balcony. The sun shone outside as a galleon passed by on the ocean. I had two glasses of champagne ready, and I called to my husband to come and join me for some fun.

"I can't," he replied, "I'm watching *Tom and Jerry*."

~ **Karen, West Sussex**

I'd asked so many times that he didn't do this, but I eventually cracked when, for the umpteenth time, rather than go home, change and pick up his car, my boyfriend came round to take me out straight from work, in his van, with the ladder on top.

I'm not a van and ladder type of girl. I just cringed getting into the damn thing. It had to end.

~ Cerys, Newport

One boyfriend was very excited when I went over to see him. He said he'd got a surprise, and I was to close my eyes, and hold out my hands.

I did so, and waited with bated breath as he rummaged around in the cupboard under the stairs. He plonked something heavy into my hands and told me to open my eyes.

"Isn't it great?", he exclaimed, "I've got a racing helmet – at last!"

I realised it was the final straw – after three years together if he genuinely thought that would excite me – we were never going to make it.

~ Caroline, Newcastle

I was really looking forward to going on a 10-day break with my boyfriend Carl, as we'd been having a bad patch, and I was sure this would fix it. When we arrived at the apartment, I was angry that the hotel had given us a twin room, but sorted it by pushing the beds together while Carl was in the bathroom.

I then went to the loo, but when I got out, Carl had separated the beds again. I was so stunned, that I didn't mention it – I was too embarrassed.

We went out for dinner later, and he drank much more than usual, so much so that when we got back to the apartment, he said he wasn't able to have sex.

In the morning, he was out jogging before I woke up (another thing he'd never done before).

After several days of him pursuing hobbies he didn't normally do and drinking like he never normally drank, it dawned on me that he was avoiding spending any intimate time with me.

When I tackled it, he said he didn't know what I meant, and that I was paranoid. Paranoid, maybe – but after 10 days of no sex and not even a kiss, I ended it when we got home – just as he'd intended.

~ **Sally, Cardiff**

SHALLOW BE THY NAME

It's all about them....

Paul's nightmare woke him. But then he looked around and realised it was OK. There were mirrors in his house, after all...

I feel shallow for admitting this, as Tim was such a lovely man, and after a few fab months it really looked like things were going well.

However, as we were walking home after a nice afternoon out, I noticed that he walked with a bounce – quite a noticeable one. Once I'd spotted it I couldn't get it out of my head.

It wasn't his fault he'd had a cycling accident that had injured his calf muscle – but that was enough.

I just couldn't see myself walking down the aisle with a man who bounced! I finished it by phone the next day....

~ **Caroline, Birmingham**

I had dated Ian for 18 months (my usual cut-off period) when we went on holiday together to Lanzarote, during which time I discovered he was without doubt the vainest and most obsessive man I'd ever come across.

He used to use nail strengthener on his nails, shaved his chest and leg hair (this was 1992!!) and had more hair products than Vidal Sassoon!

I dumped him the day of our return...

~ **Becky, Bolton**

I went out with a man for a while, but he was so incredibly vain, it was off-putting. He did all the usual stuff like looking and preening himself in every shop window and talking about himself incessantly.

But it wasn't until he finally took me home, that I realised the true extent of it. This incredibly wealthy, peacock of a man, actually had a custom-made carpet, with his own face woven in as the pattern! I stayed about five minutes after that, knowing there would always be me, him and his ego in the relationship.

~ **Alex, London**

My worst experience was picking a man in a nightclub and bringing him home. It was great sex, but when my drink had worn off, I realised he was very pale and very ginger, like a hamster. Quite repulsive really.

Unfortunately, he strutted around the apartment naked, and I was horrified when he stood in the window, full-frontal stretching and showing off for the benefit of the neighbours.

Suddenly, the words were out of my mouth. I screamed, "get back from the window, Ginger Boy!"

I felt bad, and he was very offended, but I had my reputation to think of.

I've only dated dark men since.

~ **Yvonne, Dorset**

PETTY IRRITATIONS

Often starting small, these little irritations can make or break a relationship. Usually it's a case of learning to live with it – or ending up in court for murder...

Yet again, the TV remote was cited as the 'other party' in the divorce hearing.

I couldn't bear the way my boyfriend ate spaghetti. He'd curl it round the fork, stick his tongue out like a platform, and then wedge it on there, purse his lips like a gibbon, and slurp it up. Ugh!

~ **Rachel, Gloucester**

One boyfriend used to say 'smashing' at the end of every sentence, in a really high pitch.
   After two weeks, I felt like smashing his face in.

~ **Lauren, Portsmouth**

It was meant well, but if my boyfriend asked me once within a week, he asked me a thousand times what I wanted for Christmas from his parents.

I wouldn't have minded, but we'd been dating for three weeks, and it was only July!

~ **Helene, Nantes**

My boyfriend could never stand up to his father, and I hated the way he ran around at his beck and call, doing things he hated, just to please his dad.

To make it worse, he had siblings who just used to sit back and let him. I tried to talk to him about it, but he wouldn't even broach the subject.

It was then I realised he was weak and that I had to end it, knowing that, eventually, I'd walk all over him too.

~ **Lise, Berlin**

My boyfriend used to sniff or gulp after every single sentence. It annoyed me to start with, irritated me after six months and made me want to kill him after a year.

When I finished it (for a totally spurious other reason), he sniffed, gulped and twitched all at the same time.

I remembered my mother's advice that "if something bothers you before you're married, it will be ten times worse once you are," and although I felt a bitch, I knew I'd done the right thing.

– Charlotte, Bromley

Marmite caused my divorce. Not the product. But the fact my husband used it, and never, ever, put the lid back on it.

How many jars of Marmite did I drop on the kitchen floor over our time together? It was a small, but significant start to the total breakdown of our relationship.

– **Marisa, Buckingham**

Every time I cooked a nice meal for my boyfriend in the evening, he got up and used the toilet soon after.

It became an obsession with me and I began (irrationally) hating him for wasting my efforts. And then it turned to repulsion. Oh dear...

– **Lynn, Cardiff**

124

THE JOY OF SEX (OR NOT!)

Everyone's getting more, or less than you. Or doing it better than you. Or with more people. One thing's for sure – lots of people are doing it in lots of different ways... as these stories prove!

Every time Dave thought of his sex life,
he felt like tossing himself off.

Paolo was a window cleaner/rock star (guess which one he was most successful at!). He was very attractive, and looked really 'dirty', so I was looking forward to the sex.

It did happen, but I was totally put off when, at the point of ejaculation, he seemed keen not to come in me, or on me. He simply reached down by the side of the bed, slipped on a sock that he'd been wearing earlier, and did the business into that instead!

He repeated this on two more occasions and then I decided it was a bizarre obsession, and didn't want to know again.

– **Alex, Glasgow**

My boyfriend wanted to inject some spice into our sex life. I was quite happy to try new things, but was totally horrified when he suggested getting my twin sister to join us.

We're identical – what did he think he was going to get, that he didn't with me?

– **Paula, Milan**

I knew it was over, when I realised that my boyfriend made me sick – literally.

I liked him, but never really fancied him, but figured that he was kind and funny, and that would probably do.

However, when we finally made love, he emitted a really heavy, musky scent – almost like a rutting stag! The smell of him turned my stomach so strongly that I had to go and vomit in the bathroom.

I guess we weren't nature's dream match. We'd probably have had deformed babies or something, so it was for the best.

– Ali, San Francisco

In the throes of passion my boyfriend gasped, "Tracey – you're absolutely the best shag I've ever had!"

I would have been delighted... had my name not been Helen.

– Helen C, London

My new boyfriend was gorgeous, and the first time we had made love, I was very excited. I was poised for the moment of ecstasy, but as he put it in, he screamed!

Withdrawing quickly, there was blood spraying everywhere – it was horrific. Unfortunately, one of my pubic hairs had glued across my vagina and acted like a cheese-wire, sinking itself into the helmet.

He was seriously injured, I was seriously mortified, and neither of us wanted to repeat the performance with each other ever again.

~ **Caroline, Vermont**

My boyfriend was always nagging me to go with another man, and tell him about it.

Behind my back, he arranged for me to go to Wales, stay at a complete stranger's house, wear nothing but a maid's apron all weekend, and be at this man's beck and call (both sexually and around the house).

I was horrified, so he went into a huge mood, telling me that I was selfish!

~ Liz, Cornwall

My partner disappeared under the sheets to perform oral sex. Anticipating bliss I closed my eyes and waited. And waited.

Seconds later, I heard him snoring, still beneath the sheets. I knew that if I'd lost my magic to such an extent, it was surely over.

~ Jackie, Coventry

A new-ish boyfriend and I were having sex for the first time, but it wasn't going well. He kept on his socks, didn't appear to know the meaning of foreplay, and he kept losing his erection.

We battled gamely on and then he knocked over a bottle of red wine. We stopped and I raced to the kitchen to get a cloth. I walked back to the sofa, and couldn't believe it. He was completely fully-dressed – even his shoes!

I mopped up the wine stain, totally naked, looking at him out of the corner of my eye, thinking; how? Why?

I then had to dress in front of him, all the while making small talk. We sat down to watch TV, without saying a word about what had just occurred.

It was surreal, and after leaving that night, he never called again!

– Bailey, London

My boyfriend said I was selfish for not wanting anal sex – in the full knowledge that I'd had an operation for haemorrhoids just three days before!

~ **Lisa, Edinburgh**

As my boyfriend went off me (or so I realised later), he let his personal hygiene slip to the point that he really honked.

I realise now that it was a ploy to put me off him, and it worked: I will never be able to eat cheese again.

~ **Sarita, Bradford**

I don't like dogs, so could never get used to having sex with my boyfriend whilst the dog was in the bedroom.

It was bad enough when it rested its head on the edge of the bed, bouncing up and down in time to our movements, all the while with a doleful expression on its face, but the time it jumped up and tried to lick his genitals while we were doing it, was the final straw.

My boyfriend didn't even appear phased!

I finished it there and then, but as I walked out of the door, he accused me of being a prude.

~ **Sally, London**

'What's the odd lick between friends?'

134

THE
NEW TESTAMENT

Don't Be Afraid To Be Single

WAYS TO DUMP THE LOSER

Paul Simon trilled about '50 Ways To Leave Your Lover', but he missed a few out. Modern technology has moved things on a bit, so how about:

- Faking your own death. Make friends with a reporter on the local rag and bribe them to do a small piece on your tragic demise. Be sure you definitely want it to be over though. There's no room for reconciliation beyond the grave.

- Do it the good old-fashioned way: get your friend to call and say "my mate doesn't fancy you any more. She's seeing Darren from Sainsbury's, who has just been promoted to veg". (N.B. only works if you're under 17)

- Go out for a loaf of bread, join a rugby club tour and come back 16 days later, not having phoned or anything. It works for blokes!

- Record the 'goodbye, you're a twat' message and post it on youtube.com. See how long it is until his mates see it and tell him.

- Tell him you've given up the charity shags, so it's over between you for good.

- Cook a meal of all his least-favourite foods, whilst playing his least-favourite music. Talk about shoes all the way through the meal, and then finish the conversation off with "I haven't had time for a shower today, but do you still fancy some sex?" Watch the ardour die!

- Ask every one of your friends to text him a message of your choice, at a particular time. The phone will be bombarded, and he'll literally get the message.

- Write – preferably on girly paper aimed at 10 year-olds (maybe pink, with a horse rearing up on it) – and say you're having a breakdown and may possibly be in love with *The X Factor's* Chico.

- Tell him you've realised you're a lesbian. His eyes will light up. Cut this down instantly by adding, "so I'm going to grow my leg and pubic hair back and be how God intended".

- Accidentally-on-purpose let him catch you ordering steroids and hormones on the internet. Tearfully explain you've been having counselling for months, and this is the first stage in your sexual transition.

HOW TO CATCH A RAT

They'll deny it to the death (I mean, look at Shaggy. He was in the kitchen, on the floor, on the counter, and still said "it wasn't me")... No – the only way to catch out these idiots in flagrante (or whatever her name is), is to get rock-solid evidence as follows:

- Set a honey trap. Pay a female private detective (or get a mate he doesn't know) to be somewhere you know he goes. The brief is to be sexy, obvious and available. If he resists – he's a keeper. If not, make sure she's got the evidence on tape or possibly on camera.

- Phone the local Spearmint Rhino's marketing department. Tell them you work at your partner's company and you would like some complimentary tickets sent through, (to be used on a specific date). Then see: a) if your partner mentions he's going out that night at all and b) if he does, is he honest about where 'me and a few of the lads' are going.

- Or take it a step further. Learn to pole or lap dance. Get a wig and get yourself a job at the lap-dancing club. Do the same as above, and make sure it's a night you're working.

- Arrange to 'go away' for the weekend. Instead, set up surveillance from the house opposite, or from an unmarked car nearby to see who's coming and going from your home.

- Tell every really good, attractive friend you have that you don't trust him and possibly have evidence of an affair. Make it clear that if your partner ever, ever makes a pass at them, you must know. It won't affect the friendship, but you must know the truth. It's better to lose a bad partner than a good mate.

- Find out what he's been looking at on the net. If the websites contain any kind of female profiles, photos or sexy chat, he's up for it. Take over his correspondence one evening when he's out, and see where it takes you.

- Order a few dogging magazines, in an assumed name, to be delivered to your address. Open them in front of him, and say "Oh my God. How horrendous! So that's what the previous owners were up to!" Make a great show of putting them into the recycling pile, and then two weeks later, check if they're still there.

- Set up small spy web-cameras around the home – and go away for a weekend to sit and watch what he's up to on the net. Good spots to hide them are places he'd never look, like tampon boxes or the ironing basket.

- Check the call register on his mobile. If it's wiped, then worry. If he hides the phone from you, then worry again.

- Look out for changes in his normal behaviour. If he's scruffy and smartens up, it's a clue. If he starts working late (especially if he's a postman), that's also a clue. Lipstick and perfume are good old-fashioned clues, and a definite would be a stray false nail in his hair, scratches, bruises or calling you by the wrong name more than once.

- Hurried phone calls or 'wrong' numbers where nobody speaks are often clues. If he gets into the habit of taking calls in private, or closing doors when on the phone, leave a hidden tape recorder running in the corner. All you need to do is swap the tape over, and you'll get him eventually.

PLACATORY MANTRAS

And now it's over – feel free to dip into this list at leisure, and chant as many as it takes to help you into recovery mode.

- Love should not hurt long-term.

- The small penis was a problem. You can admit it now.

- It's better to be cynical than gullible.

- Independence is a commodity you should never give up lightly. You've had a lucky escape.

- Every time anyone says "there are plenty more fish in the sea," remind them that the sea is dirty, poisoned and unpredictable.

- Men lie. Men lie. Men lie.

Coming Soon in the Bible series

Watch out for more pocket-sized hilarity coming your way:

- The Rejections, Insults and Putdowns Bible
- The Cheats, Liars and Revenge Bible
- The Great Girly-friends and Wisdoms Bible
- The Foodies and Scoffers Bible

Log on to www.knowthescorebooks.com for more details or to tell us your own hilarious, shocking and unbelievable stories.